Poverty:

Three Essays for the Season.

by

Charles Porterfield Krauth

"Blessed is he that considereth the Poor."

Repristination Press
Malone, Texas

First Repristination Press edition printed in 1997.
Reprinted in 2012.

Repristination Press
P.O. Box 173
Bynum, Texas 76631

www.repristinationpress.com

ISBN 1-891469-06-1

These three Essays, which propose no more than a glance at their topics, and which have been prepared in haste under the pressure of many duties, were presented, in their original form, as an Address at the Anniversary of the Allegheny Ladies' Society for the Relief of the Poor. They were used subsequently in the pulpit. At the request of Mr. W.S. HAVEN, who regarded them as adapted for practical usefulness, and who hoped by their circulation to promote the holy objects of Christian Charity, they have been placed in his hands for publication.

DECEMBER, 1858.

4

Essay First.

The Perpetuity of Poverty.

THERE is scarcely a duty at once so imperative, and so difficult to perform rightly, as that which we owe to the poor. The questions connected with the relief, the prevention, and the cure of Poverty and Pauperism, have engaged, in an extraordinary degree, the attention not of individual thinkers merely, but of great communities, in this age of ours. Such has been the vastness of the issues involved, that some of the most stable governments in the world have felt that the very continuance of their existence depended on their ability to meet these questions. On them, in fact, some of the greatest revolutions of past centuries have hinged. It is, perhaps, not going too far to assert, that the nation which solves the problem of Poverty, grasps the secret of immortality.

There have been, indeed, dreamers, in this dreaming world, who have imagined that it would be possible to do away with poverty. Some have treated it as an absolute social evil—a disease of the State, to be removed like cholera or small-pox; others, as a crime, to be met with the severities of law, like robbery or murder. In Egypt and in Athens, beggars were treated by law as infamous; Draco punished begging with death; and in many of the ancient states, the only refuge for the poor man and his family was to become slaves. In England the first movements of law in the repression of begging were all in the direction of severity. The act of 1536 provides that "any one able to work, who shall yet ask alms, shall be whipped for the first offense, have his ears cropped for the second, and on conviction of the third, shall suffer execution of death as a felon and an enemy of the commonwealth." The severity of this act led to its abrogation in 1547. The mild statute which took its place, provided for the reduction of beggars to slavery of two years, a repeated attempt to escape from which was to be punished with death. As this law proved ineffectual, a new effort was made in the reign of Queen Elizabeth: in 1572 it was enacted that vagrants, and all others refusing to work, should "for the first offense be grievously whipped and burned through the gristle of the right ear, with a hot iron, of the compass of an inch about; for the second, should be deemed felons, and for the third, should suffer death as felons, without benefit of clergy."

The school of Malthus has proposed to prevent the birth of a class which can give no guarantee to society that it will be able to provide for itself. To remove poverty, Socialism has devised a set of new names—expecting to heal the evil by the jugglery of language; the demagogue has set forth his agrarian schemes; gifts of land by government have been demanded; mutual aid societies, and secret beneficial associations to assure life and health, have been entered into. Some have taken the ground that the true preventative would be found in an uncompromising refusal to aid the poor in any case. Shut your purse, shut your hand, shut your eyes, shut your heart—if one who could practice on this system has a heart—and sternly say, No, to every demand.—Let these miserable creatures work or die. When they see that they must support themselves or perish, they will be aroused, and poverty will vanish. Society has but to stoop down and write with her finger in the sand, "There shall be no poor," and from that hour the poor shall cease.

In the face of all such theories, it is nevertheless very clear that the poor, as a class, will necessarily always exist. The best of these plans can only mitigate the pains and ills of poverty; they cannot entirely remove **them;** still less can they remove **it.** Diminish its amount, and relieve its various features as you may, poverty will be perpetual.

The Bible allows of no Utopian visions in reference to this point. Under the Old Testament dispensation, it was declared: "The poor shall never cease out of the land;" and our Saviour says: "The poor ye have ALWAYS with you."

Experience confirms here, as everywhere, the truth of God's Word. There has been no large general community in any age or in any land, where there has not been poverty. In monarchy and republic, in aristocracy and democracy, there have been varieties in the experience, but no contradiction of it. In the beginning of social existence, even in the shepherd life, there is soon a division between those who own the sheep and those who feed them. In our aboriginal forests there was the poor Indian and the rich Indian; in Slavery itself, on the very same plantation, where everything would seem to be reduced to a dead level, where all have precisely the same supply, the same opportunity or lack of opportunity, comparative thrift and management cause some to abound, and the lack of them keeps others in perpetual want.

The sternness of ancient Paganism—the absence of all measures, either of public or private relief—the shame and suffering attached by law to poverty—would have repressed it, if severity were the secret of prevention; but the poor increased, till, by the dead weight of mere aggregation, they dragged the state to ruin.

The benefit and ample arrangements, and the spirit of tenderness for the poor which characterized the Hebrew nation, would have repressed Poverty, if gentleness in its treatment could work a perfect cure; but we have learned from the inspired records of that people, that it was not pretended that such would be the result. In the far-off ages, a prophet opening on his harp-strings deep thoughts of One who was to crown the covenant nation with its highest glory, said of him: "He shall deliver the needy which he crieth; the poor also, and him that hath no helper." More than ten centuries afterward, Messiah came, and found thousands of the class he was to bless, meeting him everywhere. He became Himself a member of it. Lowly as it was, his deep-piercing eye saw that in its regeneration is bound up the redemption of the race. He had such words as man never spoke, such works as man never wrought, such gifts as only the hand of God could dispense; but thronging everywhere, He found enough of the poor, to receive them all.

One of the first great tokens that Christianity had begun its mission in the world, was that its spirit made such provision for the poor as had never been made before, so that out of pure love the rich unprompted made the poor partakers with them. "The had all things common. Distribution was made unto every man according as he had need. Neither was there any among them that lacked." One of the first difficulties of the young Church, a difficulty which arose in this very year in which Poverty seemed to be vanquished, was to regulate equitably the ministration to the widows. The office of deacon, which, in its true use, is the guardianship of the poor, has stood in the Church for nearly two thousand years as an evidence that poverty was with the Church in her cradle, and has been borne in her arms of love to this hour; an attestation of the difficulties connected early and always with the treatment of the poor, and of the Church's high resolve to meet duty, be its difficulties what they may. For upward of three centuries, the sole fountain of relief was the spontaneous benevolence of the people of God, and pastors, deacons, and deaconesses, were the almoners of their bounty. So thoroughly was a recognition of the perpetual claim of the poor involved in the very life of the Church, that her unhappy union with the State did not suppress her consciousness of it. In her deepest hours of darkness, she reared monastery and hospital, and attached, indeed, a superstitious sanctity to poverty. The relief of the poor retained through the entire Middle Ages, the character of private and unforced benevolence, unsustained by law or tax. When the Church at the Reformation renewed her youth, one of the first subjects of her solicitude was the care of the poor. In England, free, Christian, and prosperous as she is, it is said that statistics show that there were eight hundred and seven thousand paupers receiving assistance in the last week of August of the present year. The census of the United States in 1850, showed that within the year ending June 1st, one hundred and thirty-four thousand nine hundred and seventy-two paupers had been supported in whole or in part. All Christendom—even the Church and the State on this virgin soil, uncrowded with population, and budding with plenty, has to encounter the solemn perplexities of human poverty.

No zone or clime impairs the force of the law of which we speak. In Lapland, the heard of reindeer is owned by one man, and tended by another; in the Arctic region, one has an abundant supply of blubber, and another lives on the offal of his abundance; one has a large store of skins, another hardly enough covering to keep him from perishing. The masses of snow and ice would seem to preclude much variety in the houses reared from them, yet one has a large space with its rough comfort, another creeps into his cheerless little cavern where there is none.

It was the fortune of the writer, in the providence of God, to spend a winter and spring in the West Indies, where poverty seemed to be precluded by Nature herself, if poverty ever can be precluded. How could poverty with its ills exist there? With the thermometer at 84° in the shade, in December and January, little clothing and no fuel, except a few faggots for cooking, would be wanted. Perpetual Autumn walked the round of the months, hand in hand with perpetual Spring. The fruit in vast variety hung on the trees, with no price but the plucking. The oranges gleamed among the green leaves, which no wintry wind sweeps from the boughs, and could be furnished for the merest trifle to those who did not wish to gather them. The bananas and plantains waved their long leaves, like banners of satin, around the heavy clusters bending from the centre of the plant. The cocoanut offered itself to the climber—the guava, and all the luxurious wonders whose names are hardly known out of the tropics, hung within reach of the hand of a child. The waters swarmed with fish. The native had but to drop a fish-basket in the harbor, or some inlet of the sea, and in the morning he found in it more than enough fishes to feed his family, and by the sale of the surplus could supply their other wants. Far more labor than could be taken up, was offered at large prices. Scarcely could want be less, and supply greater than here. You would say: people in such a clime could hardly suffer if they would try. Yet large Poor-Houses are found necessary in these islands; you meet beggars everywhere, bearing the unmistakable evidences of wretchedness and suffering. The very abundance which makes it so easy to secure a living, seems to foster helplessness. But not indolence alone; sickness, accident, feeble-mindedness, old age and crime, have brought poverty thither. Some of the most abject objects human eyes ever rested on, wasted by the deadly fevers of the clime, covered with festering sores, and with the scurf of leprosy, decaying before they die, can be seen crawling, or carried about the streets of St. Thomas, and the plantations of Santa Cruz.

Even in this land of ours, the home of equal rights, and removed as it is from extremes which hasten poverty, were there an absolutely equal distribution of property this day, so that no man were richer or poorer than another, not twenty-four hours would pass before there would be the two classes of rich and poor again—the line already almost as sharply drawn in some cases, as it is in any at this hour. If a universal experience can justify a universal proposition, then is it unmistakably true that the poor, as a class, must be perpetual.

Essay Second.

The Causes of Poverty.

HE who has pondered the facts connected with the perpetuity of Poverty, will not require much further reflection to lead him to perceive how manifold are the causes which must render the number of the poor very great. There is nothing in man, or about him, which may not become the occasion of poverty.

FEEBLENESS OF BODY, disease and prostration of strength, will make many poor. If there must be workers, dependent on their daily labor, then, in the nature of the case, when the ability to work is gone, there must be poverty. There is no power which averts the ordinary ills of human life from the laboring classes, though the misery entailed upon them is heightened by their dependent condition. The lowly child of toil, who is heir to nothing else, may inherit a tendency to a special disease. The sicknesses, which are the soldiers of death, quarter themselves on the houses of the poor to make them poorer. The ratio of disease must indeed be larger among the poor than among the rich, because they are more exposed, and have fewer comforts; they live in crowded, damp, unwholesome houses, in lanes reeking with filth, in cellars which are simply spacious graves, in garrets where human life is extinguished by a slow process of suffocation. The pure air and joyous sunshine, which a merciful Father gives to the evil as well as to the good, are not shared alike by the rich and the poor. Their food is in smaller quantities, is inferior in its quality, and badly prepared. The cookery of the poor often converts their food into poison. They have not medical advice promptly, for they feel a reluctance to diminish the little they have, by paying a physician, and shrink with an honorable sensitiveness from accepting his services as a charity. The poor are not nursed as carefully in sickness. To save expense, they often, in their ignorance, use some widely-advertised nostrum. The result is, that though the disease itself may not be dangerous, they are killed or disabled by quackery. There is least provision for sickness just where most sickness is sure to prevail. In Paris, thirty deaths in every hundred take place in hospitals. Not all these are cases of poverty; but neither, on the other hand, are the cases of the dying poor, who suffer for want of that which is given in the hospital, included in the statistics. But the causes which make so large a demand there, make many demands everywhere; for in addition to the accidents to which all are exposed, labor has its own special circle of contingencies. The engineer is killed by an explosion or collision, the carpenter falls from a roof and has his skull fractured, a man attending machinery has his hand caught, and his arm torn from its socket, and is disabled for life. Sickness and casualty are busy removing or reducing to feebleness the father, the mother, the elder brother or sister, on whom many depended.

The soul of the poor man is preyed upon during

sickness by thoughts of the wants of his family, and of their utter helplessness if he should be taken away. His love for his family, and his solicitude for them, aggravate his disease. The dread of death is thrown on the side of death in the balance, and he dies because he so much dreads to die.

DEPRIVATION OR DULLNESS OF THE SENSES, OR OF THE NECESSARY BODILY ORGANS, makes poverty. The "impotent folk," the blind, the deaf, the dumb, the maimed, the halt, must be comparatively helpless. Many, too, who are not devoid of the senses and organs, have yet defects in them which largely interfere with their ability to support themselves. They are not blind, but their eyes are diseased; not deaf, but dull of hearing. They have the organ, but it is shorn of its strength. Often the defect, though real, is so latent, that the sufferer finds that men will not believe that he is an unfortunate who cannot do full work, but regard him as an indolent imposter, who prefers lying to labor.

INSANITY will make cases of poverty. What can the unreasoning, the maniac, the idiot, the feeble-minded, do for themselves or for others? Go to that home of poverty, where the father wrestled with death and seemed triumphant—but the triumph was dearly bought. His mind sunk in those awful hours of delirium, to rise no more. See that poor mother, who, urged by the wants of her other little ones, exerted herself too soon after the birth of her last child. She has brought on brain fever; and in those eyes out of which she had looked so lovingly and gently before, there is a wild glare, before which they cower in terror. Look at that family in which the children are

mysteriously blighted with a fatal tendency to idiocy—
infants in helplessness, but adults in their animal needs
and depraved passions. While these things may be, must
not Poverty endure?

Is it imagined that such cases are few? Look at a few
statistics of the most favored country of the Old World.
In Great Britain, the total number actually ascertained,
of lunatics and idiots, in the latest returns up to 1841,
was between twenty-seven and twenty-eight thousand—
the ratio in England being about one to a thousand, and
in Scotland about one to every seven hundred of the
population. In 1846, more than 20,000 insane persons
were in confinement in the asylums in England, of whom
16,000 were paupers. This embraces none of those who are
confined separately, or in the care of friends. In 436 Unions
of England and Wales, the number of pauper lunatics and
of pauper idiots deemed incurable, in the returns up to
1841, was upward of 9,000. This is a statistic of insanity
limited by the smallness of the region over which it
extends, and by the fact that it embraces none but cases of
paupers—and among these only the incurable cases. The
very complications and excitements of prosperity heighten
the tendencies to diseases of the mind. In Great Britain,
insanity has more than tripled in twenty years.

In the only land on earth more blessed than
England—our own country—the census of 1850, which
cannot overstate the fact, and for many reasons must
almost certainly very far understate it, shows, by the
ascertained aggregate, that ONE PERSON IN EVERY FOUR

HUNDRED AND SIXTY OF OUR POPULATION, is either deaf and dumb, blind, insane or idiotic. Many of these hapless creatures not only cannot supply their own wants—they cannot even tell them. The motto of the London Asylum for idiots, tells the story of the whole class: "WE PLEAD FOR THOSE WHO CANNOT PLEAD FOR THEMSELVES."

PRACTICAL INCOMPETENCE makes poverty. There are those not destitute of a large measure of mind, but who do not know how to take care of themselves. The highest order of genius, the gifts which have made men world-renowned, have not always saved their possessors from wretchedness and starvation. Men whose thoughts have shaken ancient thrones, men whose words have changed the face of nations, men of the pencil and chisel, who have wrought miracles on canvas, and cut marble into immortal shapes, men who have sung the poets' highest strains or sounded the depths of philosophy and theology, have oftentimes not had skill enough to find themselves three meals a day and a bed to sleep on. The astronomer who weighs the stars may not have the practical sense of a plowboy; the author who can apparel thought in the robes of a matchless style, may not be able to provide himself with clothing. Destitute of that common sense which is indispensable in the sphere of common things, these monarchs in the realm of mind have often been objects of common charity—often have perished for want of it. Misery has brought them to the garret, the almshouse, the jail, and the dark grave of the suicide. And there is a large class in the world without their genius, but exactly like them in their practical incompetence. You may reason and grow angry with them; the prosperous man may say: "Why do they not get along as I do? They have as good opportunities as I have, it is their own fault that they do not prosper." But it is not their fault. They do not prosper, for they do not know how; it is not in them. There is as much air for the barn-yard fowl as for the eagle, and he has wings, too, but he cannot soar; a founder has fins, and there is the water for him, but he will stick to the bottom while the dolphin plays upon the top—so is there a class in this world of ours not destitute of mind, nor of a large measure of industry and of earnestness, but who never rise.

The comparative bodily weakness of WOMAN, and some false ideas connected with it, increase the cases of poverty. From one class of occupations, woman is kept back by want of the muscular strength, from another class by the refinement of her nature, from another by the selfishness of those who wish to retain a monopoly, or by the prejudices of society. The result is, that the occupations of women are, in proportion to the demand on their part for labor, fewer than those of men. These occupations are, of necessity, therefore, overstocked. It is not because of the inhumanity of employers, but because there is a surplus of workers, that the price of female labor is brought down. The poor woman consents to take half the value of her labor, for she knows that a dozen eager applicants are ready to seize what she refuses. She chooses, therefore, not between the half and the whole, but between the half and nothing. Because of these low wages, she is obliged to toil far more than she can bear, in order to support herself and those dependent on her. Late and early, she wears body and soul away: the hand fails, and heart and life sink under it.

We talk of the inhumanity with which pagans and savages treat women, but it may be doubted whether her ordinary condition among them is further below that of the men, than the conditions of a large class of laboring women in our cities is below that which is demanded by the civilization and refinement of Christian lands, as absolutely essential to meet the common necessities and proprieties of life.

Accidents and mishaps make poverty. Property is destroyed by them. The lightning, the tornado and the flood, fall upon field, forest and home. A fire sweeps down a block of buildings, the whole property of one man, and with it is consumed, unnoticed, the little frame house, the whole property of another. One has lost his much, the other has lost his little, but both have lost their all, and in an hour the rich man is as poor as the poor man.

Arrest of business makes poverty. Commercial revulsions throw men out of employment. Factories and works are stopped; rivers fall or freeze; branches of business with which alone, men, too old to learn new ones, are familiar, are superseded; machinery is introduced, and compels those who wrought by hand to abandon their callings, and the most industrious know not where to earn their bread. The very march of civilization brings with it, incidentally, new forms of poverty. A class of mind which, in a simple condition of society, takes a relatively high position, is helpless when the strength, intelligence, and enterprise of a large and cultivated community is around it. Thousands who can prosper in a new country could do nothing in an old one. A bungling mechanic, a sluggish merchant, or an incompetent physician, may get rich, if he is the only one in a vicinity; but put him where there are others in the same employment, superior to him, and his occupation is gone. The business capacity which might answer for a little village, will not answer for a great city; and the helplessness of the individual will be equally manifested, whether he goes from his quiet nook to the city, or the city, or flourishing community, comes and grows around him. Nor is the case altered, if the man was born and reared in the city, but with only the range of mind and energy to suit him for an humbler sphere. If the little man does not take refuge in the little place, or in the little position in the large place, he is destined for ruin. The law which makes cities the places to gather wealth, is identical, to a large extend, with that which renders them the theatre of poverty in its worst form—as beneath the mighty wave, which bears the strong ship onward, the fragile boat is swamped and sinks forever.

The close connection of NATIONS, the vital bond of COMMERCE, the arrangements of GOVERNMENT, incidentally bring with them the hazards of poverty. Seasons of scarcity on one side of the Atlantic are felt on the other; changes in the Old World ruin many in the New. Over-trading breaks up the capitalist and brings down the working class with him. The disproportion between exports and imports, and all mistakes in regard to duties, have tendencies, which are at first unsuspected, but which are sure to burst in devastation over a land. The working man would perhaps smile incredulously if you told him that his personal ruin is connected with great questions of policy about which he never thinks—that far away, where laws are made or executed, some plausible theory is rising like a cloud, and that out of that cloud will fall the hail which will cut to pieces the harvest of his hopes.

To increase the burden of poverty, which causes of domestic growth have placed upon us, the wretched of OTHER NATIONS come to us, as if the waves of ocean flung them on our shores. After each storm of European revolution, they are heaped, like matted and wilted seaweed, on our coast.

IGNORANCE, even where it is not vicious, makes men helpless. It precludes them from all but a few employments, and those of the lowest order, the occupations for which the least elevated are fit, and which are, therefore, overcrowded—where wages, consequently, are smaller, and more precarious, and the workers in which can make little provision for the future.

But ignorance creates VICE, and thus, in a new form, becomes the agent of misery. We are, indeed, confining ourselves to the causes of **innocent** poverty. Yet vice is not to be omitted in the enumeration, for the guilty misery of one is often the cause of the undeserved suffering of another. The guilty father is a drunkard, a pugilist, a swindler; but his family, though innocent, suffer with him.

The TREACHERY AND CRUELTY of man to man, and of man to woman, the grasping of avarice, the violation of promises, the plausibilities of villainous speculation, bring ruin into happy homes. Here a widow invests her all in some phantom stock, some swindling bank, some enterprise designed to delude—the bubble bursts, and she and her children are left helpless in the world. Here, one of the noblest of the race, with the infirmity of too generous a trust, stakes his all, and loses it, to relieve one whom he dreams to be a friend. Over the shoulder of many a man, as he has written his name on the back of that which was to be the death-warrant of all his prosperity, the grim phantom of Beggary has leaned and leered—for he knew that the fatal paper gave its indorser into his hands forever.

The rich, by inordinate expenditures, by fine horses, fine houses, and fine furniture, by fashion, and costly amusements, by gambling, by company, and by the various vices of their class, are brought to poverty. This is their guilt; but their sons reared in habits of indolence, their daughters carefully educated to uselessness, share in the woe of the downfall.

There is a domain of Poverty too sad to be gazed upon—the tears of the virtuous blind them as they try to fix their eyes upon it—the domain of the woe-begone and heart-broken, the miserable creatures who can force the loud laugh but can never smile:

"*Where Beauty falls betray'd, despis'd, distress'd,*

And hissing Infamy proclaims the rest."

IRRELIGION makes poverty. Infidelity destroys the temporal prosperity of man. FALSE RELIGION is the mother of temporal suffering. Contrast heathenism with Christianity, in their effects, as regards the ratio and character of poverty. All systems which separate religion from morality, which destroy or diminish a sense of responsibility—all so-called religion, which is not penetrated by the vital power of a pure Gospel, tends to poverty. Contrast the countries in which a pure Christianity is presented to the view, with those in which it is corrupted. Go to the lanes of great cities, and ascertain what forms of religion and of irreligion are represented in the worst classes of pauperism, and you will see evidences of the energy with which the neglect or perversion of the religious principle acts, in the production of suffering.

But why should we continue the endless task of enumerating the sources of poverty? The very laws of our existence are the laws which doom the race to dependence. The birth of a human being is, of necessity, the birth of a beggar; and the mother is, of necessity, a beggar. The child and the wife of the rich are as helpless and dependent as the poor child and its poor mother; only, in the one case there is a well-defined relief, comparatively above the reach of accident; in the other, it is vague relief, trembling in contingencies. When the child has walked the circle of human life, he comes back to the point from which he started, and is, in "second childishness," a babe again.

Infancy and old age meet together in making poverty.

So many are the sources of Poverty, that not one of our race can say, with certainty, that he may not be reduced to absolute want. No matter how rich he may be, or how prudent; no matter how secure his investments, or how multiplied the safe-guards of his property; though he may purpose in his soul, that if villainy of the deepest die becomes necessary to maintain his hold on his earthly goods, he will hesitate at no villainy—still he may die a beggar, just as thousands, equally wealthy and prudent, as strong in every way, and as desperately unscrupulous in their purposes as he can be, have come to beggary before him.

While Nature retains her present course; while Providence clouds in mystery the throne of mercy; while State, society and trade maintain their complicated relations, and err alike in their ends and in their means; in a word, while man is man, Poverty must remain, and the poor must be many.

Essay Third.

The Relief of Poverty.

To the facts which prove the perpetuity of Poverty, and illustrate its causes, the reply of some may be: We admit that there must be poor people, and that society must provide for them, but the right way is to do the whole work by a public system, sustained by taxation. If the poor will not use the provision thus made, that is their own concern; to wiser heads than ours we leave it to settle the details of this, as of any other matter of State; our taxes are large, we pay them promptly, and do not feel that we owe the subject any further consideration.

We think, however, that even on the part of such a reasoner, it will be admitted, that, whatever might or should be the case, not all the poor are, in fact, relieved by these public arrangements. In their actual working they meet the wants of an exceedingly small part of the class. An hour's walk through the city will overwhelm an observant man with the proofs of wretchedness, famine, sickness and exposure, on the one side, and of the crimes to which they tempt, on the other, which public institutions have not touched, and which there is little reason to hope they ever will touch.

We concede that some might be relieved, who are not; that the poor, to a large extent, feel in a false sense that there is a stigma connected with receiving such relief. Yet reason with them about their foolish pride, as we may, we cannot change their feelings; and if the poor should turn on us and ask whether we would not, under the same circumstances, feel and act in the same way, wed are compelled to admit that we would. When a man has on him the brand of pauperism, he looks upon his life as a hopeless failure. He gives up the dearest treasure of his human heart at the poor-house door, for above it, though invisible to others, stand clear before his gaze, the words, which Dante says are inscribed over the gates of hell:

"All hope abandon, ye who enter here."

The poor in whom any nobility of mind is left, still hope for brighter days. Even when the soul is sick with hope deferred—hope is its only medicine. If it be too sick to take that medicine, it is too sick to live. Many and striking are the proofs in God's providence, that this yearning instinct, which we call hope, does not breathe in vain in the bosom of the poorest—the neediest may be lifted from the dunghill, and set with princes.

Often the vary charm of hope has brought the fulfillment of its own visions. A charity which relieved temporary want with the secrecy and delicacy of a true refinement, has preserved to society valuable members, who, had they sunk so far, as it seemed to them, as to accept aid from a public source, would have hidden their broken hearts and humbled heads from the eyes of men forever. But hope, which is the seed of purpose, remained uncrushed, though buried, and under the warm rains and the sunbeams of a happier time, pushed itself forth into leaf, and in due season into fruit.

Though public institutions for relief are indispensable, yet they are ordinarily the most costly means of attaining the end. In the nature of the case, they are open to the hazard of being perverted by corrupt political influences. They may come to be considered as prizes of party. Their emoluments may be enlarged, so as to render them tempting rewards for the unscrupulous. Men may be paid for the mischief they have done, by putting them in a place where they can get rich by doing more. Thousands of dollars may be squandered in salaries and fees, to pay for the distribution of a few hundreds in questionable relief. Let those who have a passion for accomplishing this whole work by taxation, ponder the history of the poor tax in England. This tax was formally organized by statute in the reign of Queen Elizabeth. The burden it imposed grew steadily, generation by generation, until in 1831 it had reached the enormous sum of eight million two hundred and eighty thousand pounds sterling per annum. Whatever effect the development of resources, the invention of machinery, the extension of commerce, the changes of state, might have in other directions, they seemed to have but one on the poor-tax, and that was to increase it. Enormous abuses hung with a parasitic tenacity and fattened on the system. To relieve beggars and to pay their legal guardians, the industrious in moderate circumstances were pinched with penury. The laborious found themselves in a condition worse than that of the paupers whom they were drained to support. The inability to meet the taxes led to legal proceedings, which completed the ruin of the tax payers, and yet gave them a sad relief by transferring them from the class of the overburdened supporters to that of the beggars. This tremendous incubus has been in large part thrown off, but England does not yet breathe freely; the remembrance of that night-mare of the nation, and the fear of its return, still make her tremble.

Let the man who wishes to save his purse, be sure of this, that the wisest plans sustained by taxation, must, in the nature of the case, involve more expense than the same amount of good would involve, when done on a judicious system of private charity. If all were done by public system that might be done, and yet more, if all could be done by it for the poor that **must** be done, it is certain that without an amount of judgment and economy for which long and bitter experience forbids communities to hope, we could be forced to take upon us a yoke of taxation, to which the present yoke and all the demands of private charity together, would seem light as air.

We are far from arguing, however, against relief by public agencies, or against their being sustained by taxes, and controlled by law. We must have them, but they must be the objects of watchfulness. They cannot do everything, but they can do a great deal, if they are properly controlled. No restraint upon their tendency to abuse, is more effectual than that imposed by the active spirit of private charity.

The two systems give each other a healthy provocation, and are a safeguard against the special one-sidedness and the dangers which pertain to each respectively.

Let it not be forgotten that Poverty and Pauperism are not synonymous. The poor, as a class, do not demand charity. Their poverty, in the vast majority of cases, is not such as to make them dependent on society; on the contrary, the result of it is, that society is dependent on them. Poverty is the source of all useful labor, of the invention that comfort, and of the arts which refine men. The wisdom of the poor wise man delivers the city. As a class, the poor are more necessary than the rich. "Much more," says St. Paul, [those members of the body which **seem** to be more feeble are necessary." A few of the great of our race come from the ranks of the rich; none from the herd of pauperism; nearly all from the homes of the poor. A community could not exist where all were rich, and who would as a consequence, do only what the rich now do. Rich and poor are, in fact, relative terms; where none are poor, none can be rich, for that in virtue of which a great deal of money is wealth, is that others have not a great deal, and are seeking for more. Change the circumstances of property, and it ceases to be wealth. To Robinson Crusoe, on his island, a ten-penny nail was a treasure—the chest of gold was valueless. Take Robinson Crusoe back to England, and his chest of gold makes him a rich man; put him at a California placer, with its enormous expenses, and he is a poor man, with only enough in his chest to support him for a few months. Were there a community in which all had a great deal of property, yet in different degrees, the relative disproportion would still practically work poverty; the man of a hundred thousand would be the poor man, to one with a hundred million. Were all unchangeably rich to the same degree, and shut up to the internal resources of the community, society would either instantly come to a dead lock, or the rich would be forced to do what the poor now do. Every man would have to go bare-footed, or make his own shoes, though, where the leather, and the thread, and the materials to work, could come from, none can tell; for all being unchangeably rich, none could present inducements to others to prepare these things. Every man would have his own dinner to cook, though it would be hard to tell where the ox would be found to furnish the material, as there would be no inducement to any one to attend to grazing; or how the other parts of a meal would be furnished, as the inducement to the market man, the grocer, and the whole family of workers who now supply men with food, would be gone. The humblest necessities would rest upon each man, and the whole be made insufferably heavy by the want of that skill which is now produced by the division of labor. All public enterprises would, of course, be an unknown thing, and the whole community would go back to something below barbarism. Where the chasm is greatest between wealth and poverty, and, at the same time, the restrictions in the way of crossing it are removed, a nation will be most active. Just as money is valuable, just in proportion as its possession is an advantage, will men be quickened to effort in every department, that they may become possessors of it. Poverty, then, is the motive power of communities. The poor, not the rich, are the independent **class**. They are the main-spring of the social watch—not the part that glitters, nor the part that first meets the eye, but that which makes it possible for the other parts to accomplish their end; at once, the least costly, and the most indispensable part of the whole. Take it away, and the watch with its golden case and jeweled pivots, is but a bauble. No class gives to society so much for so little, as the poor. In no class is purer virtue found—a warmer devotion to the interests of religion—a more willing consecration of all energies tot he service of God. It is the class of apostles and martyrs, of missionaries and of confessors, of faithful ministers and heroic reformers. It has furnished a large proportion of the most eminent workers, and the most enduring sufferers for truth and God. Withdraw the poor from any great cause, and its knell is struck in that hour.

Now when the poverty of this vital class, in exceptional cases, become such as to need relief, society, by mere justice, by the simple wisdom of far-sighted selfishness, is bound to see that there be provision made for their needs. Let her once say to the hand, "Because thou are not the head, thou are not of the body, and if there be a fester on thee, I will not cure thee, but cut thee off," and she will soon discover where the head and body would be, without the hand.

Say now, without distinction, to this class in the hour of their need: "God, where our taxes have made provision for you," and mark the result. The basest, who are worn out in crime, to whom shelter and a regular supply of food have become more desirable than full freedom to indulgence in vice, will go with willingness to the poor-house, if they cannot have their first choice, which is the jail. The utterly helpless will be compelled to go. But will that poor widow, whose heart beats high with all a mother's hope for her children, will she go with them to the alms house, and help to brand them with what she considers, and knows the world will consider, as eternal infamy? Rather will she work, and starve till she dies. That stalwart man, thrown for a time out of employment, and eagerly seeking it but not finding it, will he go thither with the wife of whom he is as proud as you can be of yours, and with his children whose faces are as fair and whose smile is as sweet to him as those of your little ones are to you? Be careful when you say to him, "As you can find no work, and your family is starving, you had better go where provision is made for paupers;" if you value your personal safety, have your retreat well planned before you say this to him.

Practice on this system, and many of the poor will be driven to desperation and crime. They will not go to the poor-house, and as on your plan every one would refuse to relieve them, they would come to an open war with society. They would rob your houses and burn them; they would take your purses and your lives. A French writer on the questions connected with Poverty, has entitled his book, "The Dangerous Classes," and among these classes are the poor, when intense suffering and a sense of cruel neglect have nursed in them all the demon passions of the human heart; when desperate with want, and inflamed by the arts of demagogues, they go forth demanding labor or bread. Such critical periods have appeared at times to be approaching even our own shores. Nothing but the general conviction felt by the poor, of the humanity and sympathy of society, has deprived such risings in our country of the infinite power of mischief they have had in other lands.

But if public agencies were able to accomplish every thing in the way of outward relief, and the poor actually accepted them, still would the blessing which our Heavenly Father has designed to connect with Poverty, thus be lost alike to the relieved and to the reliever. The strongest bonds which hold man to man would not be woven; some of the tenderest affections of the human heart would dry up by disuse; poverty would become the badge of degradation, and cease to be the incentive to action; the poor would be thankless, because they would see no connection between their relief and the sympathy of society; the rich man would forget his human brotherhood with the poor, would read no more the solemn lessons of their presence among men, the lessons which now so healthfully disturb him in his dangerous tendency to forget the hollowness of temporal good, and the uncertainty of earthly possessions. The relief which a system of taxation affords, neither excites the sense of benevolence on the one side, nor of gratitude on the other. Were it the sole system, the poor would be as the flint, with the rich as the steel, and the sparks of hatred and the kindling of malignity would be the perpetual result of their collision. The individual consideration of the poor, then, is as much needed by us as it is needed for the poor. The Bible declarations are almost always addressed to the individual, and are designed to hold the rich man and the poor man together, heart to heart. "Blessed is **he** that considereth the poor." "**He** that giveth to the poor lendeth to the Lord." "**Thine** alms have come up as a memorial." "**Thou** when **thou** doest thine alms." "**Thy** Father shall reward **thee**." There must then be **private** charity, and by this we mean charity dependent on the **voluntary** act of the individual. An institution, however extensive, if it be sustained by voluntary gifts, by annual contributions, or by individual endowment, is a **private** charity. The aid of the State, provided it be not such as to make the institution dependent on the State or subject to its control, does not take from it its character as a private charity. Every charity not sustained by law, nor deriving its revenue from a tax, is a private charity.

Yet while there must be a private charity, of all its modes, **indiscriminate** giving to every one who asks is the worst. To give indolently and carelessly increases poverty just in the ratio to the profusion with which it is done. Street begging is a burden to the rich, but it is an unspeakable curse to the poor; it makes liars and thieves of the worst class of the poor, and increases the difficulties of the deserving.

Neither on the other hand, however, is **indiscriminate refusing** of all who ask, justifiable, unless we carry out some good plan by which the really needy shall be found out; for if we will not give at all lest we should give to the unworthy, and will not seek for the worthy, we force the poor to beg or perish—or in fact, on this plan, to beg and perish. Knowing what human nature is, we are **driving** them to crime, just as the other plan **lures** them to it.

Our charity, removing itself from each of these extremes, is to be broad, yet full of intelligent discrimination. The poor of the "household of faith" are to be relieved within the Church, promptly, and with all the refinement of Christian sympathy. This is to be a family matter—something between brothers and sisters. This done, we are to go forth in the wide field of society to do good on a larger scale "to all men." This is the sphere of charity. The field in which she sows her alms, like seeds of blessing, is the world.

For what are "alms," and what is "charity?" The word "alms" was first employed in the German Church usage, and has passed into almost every Christian language. It is simply the contraction of the Greek word for "mercy;" which is always, in the New Testament, used in the sense of "alms." "Alms," then, are gifts or deeds of "mercy." "He that hath **mercy** on the poor, happy is he." There must be the prompting of pity, or there can be no true alms. If you have no money, loving words and tender acts are alms. The meaning of charity is love. It takes its stamp from something within the man. St. Paul supposes a case, which, on the popular misapprehension of charity, (a misapprehension which would confer that sacred name on the cold and careless gift of a trifle to a beggar, to get rid of him,) is a very absurd one: "Though I bestow all my goods to feed the poor, and have **not** charity, it profiteth me nothing." Charity is a quality of the heart, not a detached act of the hand; it prompts the hand, and hallows its deed. The **sympathy** which prompts healing words and gentle ways, is dearer to the poor man than meat or money. Give him what else you may, he feels that in **it** lies the true charity. You fling a few coppers at a mendicant; he picks them from the mud, and curses you internally while he does so. The bread he buys with them relieves his hunger, but the man is not relieved. His soul is sadder and sorer; he has less of its treasure of kindliness and hopefulness than he had before. Your gift has made him poorer than ever. You are not his benefactor; you are his robber. True charity is considerate mercy; it benefits the right persons. It is not, on the one hand, frightened into compliance with the demands of insolent mendicancy; nor does it, on the other, fail to relieve the humble and the truly needy, because they shrink from making their wants known. For true charity SEEKS its objects. It "GOES ABOUT, doing good." It relieves at once, for it will not add to the pains of poverty, the agony of suspense. It is thoughtful, and therefore gives the right sort of relief, in the right way. Some charity is pure blundering walking about under the mantle of good intentions, hurting people for love of them. True charity is not mere well-meaning profusion, without examination. It will not send the right things to the wrong people, nor the wrong things to the right people. A man may spend, and scatter, and waste a fortune, without fulfilling the real ends of benevolence. Nobody is the better of it all. True charity is at once abounding and economical. It does not feed the hungry on delicacies, but on simple and healthy food, and feeds them well. But makes the barley loaves and fishes go as far as possible, and gathers up the fragments, that nothing be lost. It will feed five thousand with the provision which a badly administered law might make for a few pampered officials. Charity is patient. It seeks long, and when it finds itself mistaken, is not deterred from trying again. It does not give up a good work because it cannot be done in a day. It bears with the short-sightedness of the poor, which often makes them exacting and ungrateful to their best benefacts. It is steadfast. It does not allow itself to be carried away by novelty, then sink into indifference, and require to be aroused by artificial stimulation; but goes from strength to strength, in a daily advance, on the pathway of duty. It is, in the true sense, radical. It goes, where it can, to the root of the evil, and labors to prevent its growth, as well as to relieve its ills. It exercises a wise caution, so as not to encourage indolence or dependence. It does not work planlessly, but on well devised systems; not in isolation, but in coöperation. It is not smitten with the ambition of seeming to do everything, but divides, that it may conquer, and declines many things, that it may accomplish much. It shapes its course after the right example; not that of a pretentious, and often infidel show of concern for men's bodies, which tacitly assumes that they have no souls, but in lowly conformity with that divine life which was made manifest in the flesh, as the guide of ours.

This is the charity which rears the hospital, and nurses its sick and friendless inmates. When ungrateful governments forget the war-worn soldier, she finds him a peaceful home; when Commerce abandons the sailor who can serve her no more, she finds him a harbor where the sea-beaten hulk shall lie safe from wind and wave. Like the Divine One who breathed her into being, she knows not Greek nor Jew, bond nor free—no clime, no color, no religion, no sex; she sees the lineaments of a common Father in the duskiest visage, and hears the accents of brotherhood in the uncouthest tongue. The poor immigrant, come whence he will, she welcomes. Whom Christ died to redeem, she lives to bless. Like the sunbeam which descends and slants through the window pane of the chamber of suffering, she comes down from heaven and enters the sick room to brighten all she touches. She cools the parched lips of fever, and flies to the side of the wasting consumptive, as his hollow cough breaks in on the stillness of the night. She provides for the mother and the child, for the fatherless and motherless, and the widow. Charity doe snot fear contagion, nor the loathsomeness of disease. She takes into her care those from whose "sore" friend and lover, wife and sister, have fled in terror. She searches for hope in the eye of the blind, and when that hope fails, teaches him to see with his fingers; she interprets her soul of sweetness to the deaf, and teaches the dumb an eloquence beyond that of words; she lifts the lame and sends him into the Beautiful gate of the temple, "walking, and leaping, and praising God." What is too loathsome for mere humanity to touch, she lays tenderly upon her bosom. She strives to wake up the dormant reason and the slumbering affections in the lunatic and idiot. She has medicine for the sick, food for the hungry, garments for the suffering, and health and comfort for the homes of the poor. She is humble enough to do the lowliest offices, and has faith enough in God to undertake the greatest. Ask who placed the warm little socks on the feet of that poor babe, the reply is, Charity. Ask who reared those mighty houses of relief— in building which millions were expended—in sustaining which hundreds of thousands are spent annually—the institutions of which kings are proud to be nursing fathers, and of which great nations make their boast—who reared them? and the reply is, Charity. Often, indeed, it is the most glorious angels of her presence, those who do **always** behold her face, who have the lowliest cares, and are the guardians of the least among the little ones whom she loves. It may be some seraph spirit of her sending, which hands over the forsaken in that ministration of mercy of which none but the sufferer and God shall ever know; while the promptings of one of the furthest removed of her angels, of one whose wings perhaps were not totally unsoiled with the love of the praise of man, led to the munificent gifts whose trumpeting fills the world's ear, and whose results are seen in some vast palace for the poor, which gives the name of its founder to eternal fame.

But true Charity has a grander sphere than all of which we have spoken. She looks at the immortal nature of the unfortunate, sees that the most awful feature of poverty is, that it is a lure to the soul, seducing it to crime, is linked with vice which aggravates all its horrors. She educates, therefore; she trains, she shields, she preaches the Gospel to the poor, she upholds the sinking, and tenderly lifts the fallen. Those whom society has hissed from its presence, she strives to redeem; she searches for the jewel amid the wreck of the casket. The erring Magdalen, who looked at mankind with a brow which seemed all brazen and defiant, has wept at her feet, has felt her gentle and pitying hand on her drooping head, and strengthened by her voice of love, has learned to sin no more. She is a mother to the foundling, and a nurse to the aged; she saves the young offender by finding him a place of refuge from the dread temptations which would harden him into an irreclaimable criminal; and hoping against hope, she presses to the jail, the penitentiary, the scaffold, on her mission of love. She gives and endows; she has her week, her day, her hour, her constancy in season, her promptness out of season. She follows the plan of the beneficence of the Highest, which is not to do good fitfully and at random, but to put the exercise of mercy under the law of order. She is ever meek, save when human applause strives to draw from her one look of regard. Then is her heart moved to disdain; and when on the eve of some surpassing sacrifice toward which she has set her face, selfish love whispers, "Be this far from thee;" then the lightning of a griefful indignation breaks forth from her holy eyes, and she says, "Get thee behind me, Satan."

Look on her face, so seraphic, yet so serene and

tender,—so beaming, yet with a gentle tinge of solicitude softening its radiance. There is in it a sadness transfigured, a grief melting into heavenly light, such as shines on but one face. Are your eyes holden, that they know it not? It is the very face of CHRIST. He is gone—yet lo, he is here always, dwelling in the faithful and the holy. Oh, if Christ, the suffering, Christ, the hungering and thirsting, the naked and sick, the stranger and prisoner, still abides on earth in the person of those who suffer, abides in their persons because His love makes Him one with them,—Christ the pitying and relieve moves among men in the person of those who pity and relieve, moves in their persons because His grace makes them one with Him. As the burdened and sorrowing "fill up that which is behind of the afflictions of Christ," so do the loving and helping become channels of that stream of His love which yet remains to be poured upon the world through every age, filling up that which is behind of the benedictions of Him who ascended on high that He might give gifts unto men. Charity has gazed on the incarnate Mercy, and love, and followed, and given herself up to His transforming power, till she has been changed into His very image. He who would know how Christ looked, must not go to the dim imaginings of the painter or of the statuary, but must fix on her his eyes, and learn from her what was the marvelous beauty of Him who was "fairer than the children of men."

Need we speak of the blessings which such a visitant brings to the heart of those who receive her? She is herself her own blessing. Whatever she may bring to the poor, great as its blessings may be—and its blessings are priceless—it is little compared with that which she brings to him in whose bosom she dwells. When the widow's heart is singing for joy, it is sweet to hear the music of her gladness in the grateful words in which she thanks her benefactor; it is sweet to read in the eyes of those who are desolate no more, what they struggle in vain to utter with their lips; but there is something sweeter, which fills in the pauses of our busy hours, something which beautifies our brightest moments, and mitigates our saddest. It is like a sky-lark in our sunshine, and a nightingale in our darkness, singing all day and all night, but loveliest in the night. Led by the hand of a pure charity, that sister angel ever enters the soul. That angel of the heart is a happy conscience, testifying of the approval of our God. Sweeter even than the song of the poor, is its song. He, in whom a heaven-illumed conscience dwelt, like the fullness of the God-head bodily, has declared:

"It is more blessed to Give than to Receive."

www.ingramcontent.com/pod-product-compliance
Lightning Source LLC
Chambersburg PA
CBHW071751020426
42331CB00008B/2270